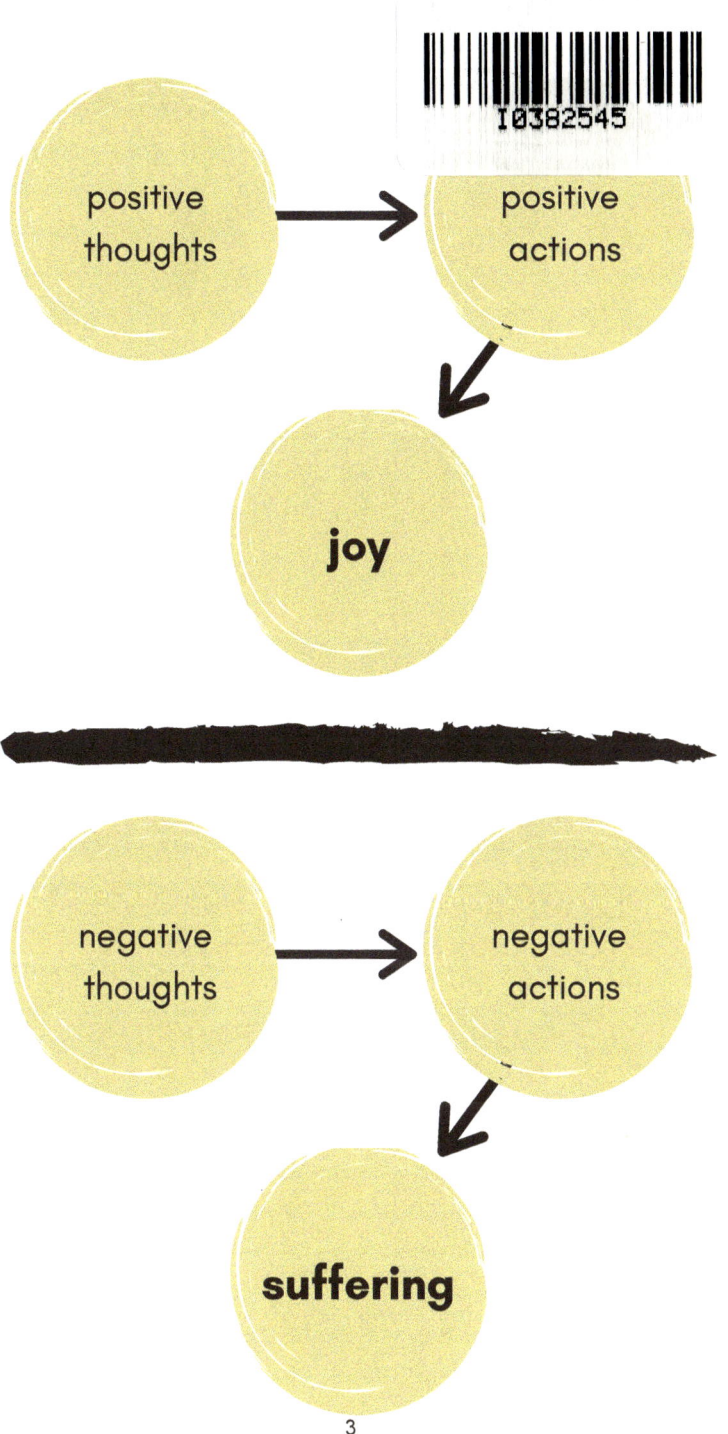

Say it Loud!

I am what I THINK I am.

The Black Manifest is a daily self-workbook for black men that includes writing prompts, affirmations, and intentions to help improve your overall well being.

This is for the black man whom may not know how to say it.
Write it down and work it through.

This is for the black man whom may not know what to say.
There is power in the tongue.
Speak power, peace, and prosperity into your life.

This is for the black man that may not know where to start.
It begins and ends with you, your mind, and your thoughts.

This is for the black men in my life.
I see you. I value you. I love you.

What do you see?

Gentleman A: A long road leading to nowhere. Trees and leaves and nowhere to go.

Gentleman B: A nice scenic route. A peaceful getaway. A long road with adventures ahead.

P E R S P E C T I V E

Who are you?

Write about the man you see yourself to be.

Say it Loud!

I am enough.
___

What is your favorite quality/characteristic about yourself?

pur·pose

noun

the reason for which something is done or created or for which something exists.

King,
Everything has purpose,
including you!

Be Intentional

Today, I will walk with purpose. I will move confidently knowing that I belong. This moment and every moment that I am given will be used purposely, in a positive way, for the benefit of my life.

Say it Loud!

I have the power to transform myself.
I can change.

What is one habit that you would like to change?

I will change

> I smoke, I drank, I'm supposed to stop but I can't

— BODY HEAD BANGERZ

lies, all lies
YOU CAN STOP!

We are taught that we should keep our pain to ourselves and that it will pass. So, we suffer in silence and self medicate to cope. The truth is that we can not move pass it unless we work THROUGH it

YOU CAN STOP.

Now is the time to unlearn and relearn.

Change your mindset and your thoughts and you will change your life!

What do you do to cope with challenges in your day to day life?

_____
_____
_____
_____
_____
_____
_____
_____

Ask yourself, is this a healthy way to cope?

_____
_____
_____
_____

If not, what are some healthy alternatives you can try?

For example: When I feel anxious and overwhelmed, I drink. I realize that this is not the healthiest way to cope. Therefore, I will now try 30 minutes of cardio on days when I feel anxious or overwhelmed.

Your turn!

healthy ways to cope

No matter how full the river, it still wants to grow.

-AFRICAN PROVERB

King,
we are constantly evolving beings. Always look for ways to improve your life. Keep growing!

Say it Loud!

I give myself permission to do what is best for me.

**What is right for you may not be popular or acceptable to others.
What do you need the most right now?**

> we fill our lives with noise to drown out our sorrows.

— CINN WRIGHT

SET A TIMER FOR FOUR MINUTES

find a quiet place to sit or lie comfortably with your back straight

close your eyes

INHALE slowly
through your nose
for a count of four

hold for a count of two

EXHALE slowly
through your mouth
for a count of four

REPEAT

Be Intentional

I give myself permission to own every room I enter today. I will show up fully and wholly. I will be present for myself and for all those that I have committed myself too.

—

SHOW UP AND SHOW OUT!

Say it Loud!

I am a good man/husband/partner/friend/brother/son.

Which relationships in your life do you feel are going really well right now?

Why?

Which relationships in your life do you feel needs improvement?

Why?

What relationships in your life do you feel are not good for you and should be let go?

Why?

Say it Loud!

I give love and
I deserve love.

Write about the first person that comes to mind when you say LOVE.

What is your greatest memory of this person?

DUMP IT

This exercise is most commonly known as free writing but, I call it "dump it"

You will set a timer for two minutes, and write continuously whatever comes to mind. Do not worry about grammar.

It is kind of like when you free style rap. You say whatever comes to mind. Except, you write it on paper and it does not have to make sense.

You simply write any and everything that comes to mind. You take all of your current thoughts and "dump it" onto the paper.

You leave with a clear mind and a clear start to your day.

> **Free your mind and your ass will follow**

— MORGAN FREEMAN,
BRIAN BANKS

What healthy hobbies do you have that make you most happy?

schedule some time this week to do this hobby!

too many men in cycle of jail spending they birthdays inside of a cell. We come from a bloodline of trauma we raised by our mamas
Lord we gotta heal

- J.COLE, MIDDLE CHILD

Is there any childhood trauma that you are still healing from?

King, just by acknowledging this is a step in the right direction.

unhealed childhood trauma

can manifest itself in your life daily as any or all of these traits:

ANXIETY
CHRONIC FATIGUE
DEPRESSION
CO-DEPENDENCY
PLAYING THE VICTIM/BLAMING
PEOPLE PLEASING
FEAR OF ABANDONMENT
PASSIVE AGGRESSION
NEGATIVITY
TOLERATING ABUSIVE BEHAVIOR
BEING ABUSIVE
DIFFICULTY SETTING BOUNDARIES
ATTRACTING NARCISSIST
BEING A NARCISSIST
PUTTING OTHERS NEEDS BEFORE YOUR OWN

Does any of these traits resonate with you? Write each one.

_____
_____
_____
_____
_____
_____
_____
_____
_____
_____
_____
_____
_____
_____
_____
_____
_____
_____
_____
_____
_____
_____
_____

This self-workbook is a great first step to recognizing where you are mentally. Therapy/counseling may be the next step to helping you work through the above.

Son: Mommy, Please sleep with me tonight.

Mom: Sure, okay!

WAKE UP

Mom: Good Morning. Did you sleep good?

Son: Yes, I felt safe.

What makes you feel the most safe?

Why?

What is something you have always wanted to say to your mother?

What is something you have always wanted to say to your father?

I have a magic wand. Name an event or experience in your life that you would like for me to delete?

_____
_____
_____
_____
_____
_____
_____
_____
_____
_____
_____
_____
_____
_____
_____
_____
_____
_____

First, rip this page out. Now, close your eyes. Imagine this paper represents this memory. Now, tear it into tiny pieces. Finally, throw it in the trash. This is a representation of letting it go.

every day

is a new opportunity to begin again. Your past does not define you. Who and what you are right now is what matters most!

your manhood

is not measured by the measurement of your "man hood". The measurement of your penis does not determine your self-worth. Your self-esteem level should not be directly tied to the measurement of your penis.

Every mans penis is big to someone. Every mans penis is small to someone. Size does matter to some and size does not matter to others.

Do you quit searching for a job because an employer does not like you and chooses not to hire you?
No, Exactly! You find a company that is a better fit for you.

Do not feel less of who you are because of the opinions of others.

there, I said it!

It needed to be said!

> **vulnerability creates transparency**
>
> — CINN WRIGHT

What is a hard truth you would like to tell someone?

Be as transparent as possible.
There is no one here but you!

HOL' UP
WAIT A
MINUTE

Let this marinate for a moment.

"vulnerability creates transparency"

Do you know what it means to be vulnerable? In short, it means to be open. To bare yourself and let your true self, thoughts, and feelings be seen.

When you are courageous enough to be vulnerable with others then, you have transparency.

This, in turn, creates the most open and honest connection with yourself and those you are in relationship with.

King, think on that. However, if you choose to write on it, I left you some space on the next page.

SPACE

SPACE

Be Intentional

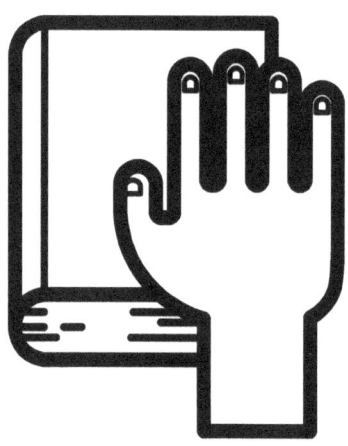

Today, I will stand in my truth with myself and all those that I encounter.

—

Write the name of at least one person you will be open and honest with today. Tell them something you have always wanted to tell them.

Name:

I really need you to know that

Say it Loud!

I am in the process of becoming the best version of myself.

What are you most proud of yourself for?

> One man can not make a team.

— KAREEM ABDUL JABBAR

Do you have a brotherhood? Name one man that you can confide in about your journey to "Gettin' Your Mind Right"?

_____
_____
_____
_____
_____
_____
_____
_____
_____
_____
_____
_____
_____
_____
_____
_____
_____
_____
_____
_____
_____
_____

Black men have to hold each other accountable. As brothers, you have to empower one another and be willing to let each other know when there is room for improvement.

ask for help

It is okay to ask for help. Asking for help is NOT a sign of weakness. You do not have to do it all alone.

Is it hard for you to ask for help? Why or why not?

> it's just me against the world, got nuttin' to lose

— TUPAC

What has it been like for you being a black man in America?

Say it Loud!

I matter.
―――――――――――

Read with confidence

I matter. My opinions matter. My thoughts matter. I matter. My mental health matters. My heart matters. My feelings matter. I matter. My intentions matter. My voice matters. I matter. My life matters. My effort matters. My choice matters. I matter. My opinions matter. My thoughts matter. I matter. My mental health matters. My heart matters. My feelings matter. I matter. My intentions matter. My voice matters. I matter. My life matters. My effort matters. My choice matters. I matter.

I MATTER

emancipate yourself from mental slavery. none but ourselves can free our minds.

— BOB MARLEY, REDEMPTION SONG

Mental health and therapy seems to carry a stigma within the black community. What are your thoughts on therapy?

therapy

is basically the gym for the mind. Just as we work out and eat properly to keep the body healthy, we also need therapy to keep the mind healthy.

According to therapyforblackmen.org Suicide is the third leading cause of death for African American males ages 15 to 24.

Among men aged 18—44 who had daily feelings of anxiety or depression, non-Hispanic Black and Hispanic men (26.4 percent) were less likely than non-Hispanic White men (45.4 percent) to have used mental health treatments.

Keeping a journal, meditation, physical activity and, even a walk in nature can assist in managing daily stress and anxiety. Learning to manage stress, anxiety, and depression will help to improve your overall mental health. If you have made it this far in this workbook you have already checked off journal and meditation.

Then, there is good old fashion talk therapy.
I mean who would not want to spill all of their problems, worries, anxieties, questions, and desires to a certified mental health professional with an unbiased opinion who will listen judgement free? Sign me up!

King,
I'm just saying...it is definitely food for thought.

Say it Loud!

I am powerful beyond measure.

**Sometimes, we tend to fear our own greatness.
As the saying goes, fear is just
False Evidence Appearing Real.
What is one thing you have always
wanted to accomplish?**

_____
_____
_____
_____
_____
_____
_____
_____

Write a game plan to get it done in the shortest time possible. Make it S.M.A.R.T (Specific, Measurable, Achievable, Realistic, Timely)

Writing it all out step by step is an essential part of manifesting it.

You can do this!

THE

GAME PLAN

YOU DID GREAT!

You have your game plan! It is important that you remain focused, motivated, and consistent. Do not give up on yourself!

21 Days of Affirmations

It is said that it takes twenty-one days to create a habit. I have provided you with 21 affirmations on the following pages. For the next 21 days, say the affirmation for that day at least twice or all throughout the day. These daily affirmations will help motivate, inspire, and encourage you to move your life in a positive direction. Speak them confidently and with certainty. DO NOT speak these affirmations absentmindedly.

DAY ONE:
Say it Loud!

My life changes with my mindset and my thoughts.

DAY TWO:

Say it Loud!

I am powerful beyond measure.

DAY THREE:

Say it Loud!

I deserve happiness and success.

DAY FOUR: Say it Loud!

I am intelligent. My mind is full of brilliant ideas.

DAY FIVE:
Say it Loud!

I grow and learn valuable lessons every day.

DAY SIX:

Say it Loud!

I am a great provider.

DAY SEVEN:

Say it Loud!

I have the courage to keep going.

DAY EIGHT:

Say it Loud!

I bravely strive to better myself.

———

DAY NINE: Say it Loud!

I am strong. Even on days when it does not feel like **I am**.

DAY TEN:

Say it Loud!

I forgive myself.

DAY ELEVEN:
Say it Loud!

I confidently move through obstacles instead of avoiding.

DAY TWELVE:

Say it Loud!

I am destined for greatness.

DAY THIRTEEN:

Say it Loud!

I am wealthy.

DAY FOURTEEN:

Say it Loud!

I am worthy of greatness.

DAY FIFTEEN: Say it Loud!

I am strong mentally, physically, and spiritually.

DAY SIXTEEN:

Say it Loud!

I am deserving of all good things.

DAY SEVENTEEN:

Say it Loud!

I am the hero of my story.

DAY EIGHTEEN:

Say it Loud!

I am in charge of my own happiness.

DAY NINETEEN:

Say it Loud!

I am not in control of others.

DAY TWENTY:
Say it Loud!

My dreams are possible. **I am** full of potential.

DAY TWENTY-ONE:

Say it Loud!

I have a lot to be grateful for.

———

Now, try creating some affirmations of your own.

Now, try creating some affirmations of your own.

Dear Black King,

I see the weight that you carry on your shoulders. I see the battles that you are silently fighting. I want you to know you don't have to do it alone. I want to support you by motivating you to take care of yourself mentally, physically, and spiritually. You possess the courage to prioritize your mental and physical health. This does not make you weak. This amplifies your strength and I call you King as a reminder of your courage and your strength.

Love,

A Black Queen

www.ingramcontent.com/pod-product-compliance
Lightning Source LLC
Chambersburg PA
CBHW042128100526
44587CB00026B/4219